I CAN BE WHOEVER

I WANT TO BE

By Nigel Robinson

Table of Contents

Preface

This book was written to inspire our children to be whoever they want to be in life. I strongly believe that our children are the future and we must invest in their psychological growth in order to cultivate greatness in them. Growing up as a child I can clearly remember messages conveyed by colorful books that fueled my imagination. If we can capture the imagination of the youths, then even in their adult years they will remember the books they read as a child that inspired them to be the greatest. I would love this book to be one of the books that stays with a child through all the developing years of their life. I encourage parents and all adults in our community to get involved in the lives of our children who are the ones who will shape our future. Occupy them with inspirations like these and watch them flourish.

I can be an engineer if I want to be. Programing computers and building things would be all fun to me. I would create things that everyone would love. Creating machines that travels below and travels above. I would design a spacecraft that lands on the moon. I would create ships that can sail around the world before high noon. Being an engineer would be the coolest thing ever. I would make planes that can fly through any weather.

I can be a doctor if I want to be. Healing people is my specialty. Keeping my patients healthy and fine, eating right and exercising on time. Helping mothers give birth to healthy newborn babies is the goal. Seeing my patients smile would greatly warm my soul. Learning to be patient and well disciplined, will show my patients that my intentions are genuine. Curing cancer and diseases is my aim, as well as mending hearts and fixing brains. I can work for insurance companies, in hospitals, clinics and hospice. I can cure different patient's diagnosis by running elaborate diagnostics.

I can be an astronaut if I want to be, I would fly to every galaxy. Orbiting planets and orbiting stars, going to solar systems near and far. I want to be the first to go to another universe, to see if there are other inhabitable planets just like ours. If there are other people out there like me, it would be something interesting I want to see. I will take my space shuttle to places that are far, places like Venus, Jupiter and Mars. I would take my mother, father, brothers and sisters with me, just so they can experience the beautiful things that I see. Our universe is a part of the galaxy called the Milky Way. It's called the Milky Way because it looks like a milky circle from far away.

When I get older I want to be an educator. I want to learn and teach my true history before we crossed the equator. My people are indigenous to every piece of land. I want to teach people about our greatness before others came along. I want to teach everyone that all the things that are taught in school originally came from Africa. Things like philosophy, math, biology, hygiene, medicine, astronomy and navigating the entire planet all the way to Antarctica. My people are Kings, Queens, royalty and warriors. My people are also discoverers and inventors. I want to teach my people to come together, as brothers and sisters and love each other.

I can be an Architect if I want to be. I would build the best buildings and structures there will ever be. Everyone will depend on me to create a plan. I can build a small model of a large building so everyone can know where it will stand. I can create blueprints to show buildings on a smaller scale. This will show everything about the building to the smallest detail. As an architect, I can reconstruct and rebuild my community. I can design buildings for people to have fun and festivities.

I can be the president if I want to be. I will attend law school after I get an undergraduate degree. When I govern my people, they will be very thankful, because knowing the laws of the land is very helpful. I will get the highest grade in school because being the president is very cool. It is the highest honor in the world, and I can better help every little boy and every little girl.

I can be a physical therapist if I want to be. I will be helping people regain their physical abilities. I will help strengthen their legs and strengthen their arms, keeping them in tip top physical form. I can help people heal from their injury, without using drugs or any surgery. I will offer massage, heat treatment and exercise, because my healing techniques are very precise.

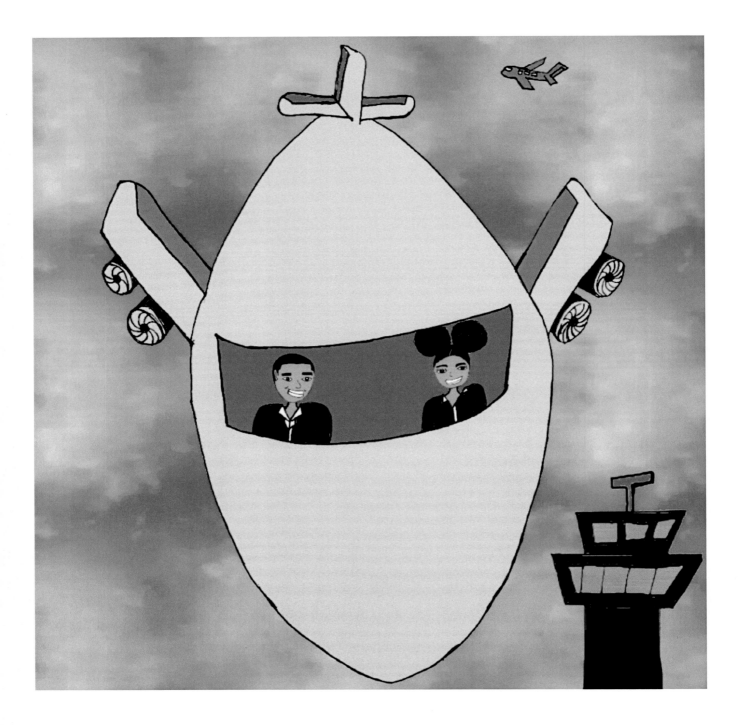

I can be a pilot if I want to be. I will fly around the world faster than a bumble bee. Safely delivering passengers wherever they want to be, because I am the safest pilot there will ever be. I will fly proudly in the deep blue sky, watching beautiful sunsets from a high. I will fly to places near and far, from Timbuktu to Madagascar. I will fly across all 7 continents, while my passengers enjoy the beautiful view to their hearts content.

I can be an author if I want to be. I will write hundreds of books for everyone to read. I will write books for cooks, lawyers, doctors and engineers, I will write novels and short stories about lions, tiger and bears. I will write more books and plays than Shakespeare, I will write books about places everywhere. I will write so many books for you to read, you won't finish them all even if you read at the fastest speed. I can write books that are filled with mystery, suspense and with fame. I can write books that you will read at nights by the brightest candle flame.

I can be a top designer for models, celebrities and everyone. I will design as much unique clothes as I can. I will be as creative as I can be, so everyone will love to wear my pants, skirts, blouse, and tees. I will design clothes for the president and everyone across all 7 continents. I will design clothes that are very stylish. I will make clothes that are very rich, luxurious and lavish. I will make clothes that are very affordable as well as expensive. This is because my talent is unique, and my work is very intensive. As a designer, I must know my neats, knife-pleats and leotards. I must know my measurements of millimeters, inches, feet and yards.

I can be a scientist if I want to be. I can study animas as a zoologist. I can study rocks and you will call me a geologist. I can also study organisms and living things as a biologist. I will solve problems using my senses of tasting, hearing, seeing, touching and smelling. I will present discoveries to the scientific community that is very compelling. I will discover ways to keep the air clean. I will invent ways to destroy sickness and diseases that are very mean. I will be observing, measuring and communicating. I will watch bacteria grow on my petri dish for cultivating. I will design new and safe chemicals, for doctors and nurses to use in their clinical. I will mix different compounds and different solutions. I will help to solve our environment pollution.

When I grow up I would like to be a judge. After my rulings, no one will hold a grudge. I will throw the book at criminals and vindicate those who are innocent. I will lock away people who are very mean and violent. Not all cases deserve a conviction, because I will go over all the details and additional information. In court, I will always be addressed as Your Honor. I will rule my courtroom with fairness in a respectable and graceful manner.

One day I will be a very profitable entrepreneur. Owning my business by being smart and using hard work and labor. I will invest in things like penny stocks. I will start by putting more pennies in my piggy bank around the clock. I am going to save up to buy my first investment property. I will no longer live poor and in poverty. I will open accounts on the stock exchange, to increase my profits and my business range. I will be familiar with words such as budget, profit and annuity. I will carefully manage my business equity. I will earn more money to fuel my bottom line. My family will be proud of me and my beautiful business mind. I was born to be a boss and I will accomplish this with distinction and class.

I want to be an artist when I grow up. I can draw a plane, a car or a truck. I love drawing and painting all kinds of pictures. I like to play with paint of different colors and mixtures. Artists are valuable very much, because they can create a different mood with the stroke of a brush. The movement seen in my art will be swirling, dancing, flowing and dramatic. The colors will be bold, subtle, vibrant, earthy and naturalistic. I will use different forms of geometry as well as different ways to express symmetry. Words such as curvaceous, angular and elongated will describe my work. Critiques will have fun explaining my art and my different uses of light, hues, shadows and dark.

I can be a composer if I want. I will create music for people to enjoy, move their feet and chant. I want to be a great composer like Chevalier de Saint-Georges, Florence B. Price, Samuel Coleridge-Taylor, Will Marion Cook and George walker. I love music so much I could compose music for an entire orchestra. I will make classical music and be the conductor. When I wave my hands at the musicians I am just setting the tempo. I will bring all the string, wind and percussion instruments to a roaring crescendo. I will learn musical terms such as alto, allegro, acapella and accelerando.

I can be a Movie Director if I want to be. Everyone I know loves to watch a good movie. I will be the best director ever. I will direct plays, shows, movies, actresses and actors. I will direct movies with stuntmen and stunt doubles. I will direct action movies that leave things lying in rubbles. I will direct comedy, satire, horror, historical movies, fantasy and drama. I will also direct movies such as independents, thrillers, romance, science fiction, mystery, urban, political, adventures and sagas. I can allow performers to use ad libs to improvise. It can make the movie funnier than you would realize. Anthropomorphism is to give animals human characteristics. This can give the movie plots and turns more interesting twists. My movies will never receive ratings of rotten tomatoes, because they will be so interesting it keeps the viewers on their tippy toes. I will introduce my movies to film festivals, so they can be bought for millions by companies with the highest approvals.

I Can Be Whoever I Want to Be

I can be whoever I want to be
And no one or anything in the world can stop me
I will plant my feet firmly in the ground
pursue my dreams, never holding my head down
I will be the best person I can ever be
For community, family and most importantly me
No one will ever stop me from being a dreamer
Because while they sleep I will be an over achiever
The race of life is never for the fastest person
It is for those who prepare that victory is certain
No one can tell me that I can't be great
It will only make me more determined to elevate
One day they will try to congratulate
But I will look at them because it's way too late
I can be whoever I want to be
And no one in all the universes and galaxies can stop me.

THE END

Made in the USA
San Bernardino, CA
16 April 2018